Warren Holden

Leaflets from Christian Thoughts

Warren Holden

Leaflets from Christian Thoughts

ISBN/EAN: 9783337264062

Printed in Europe, USA, Canada, Australia, Japan

Cover: Foto ©Lupo / pixelio.de

More available books at **www.hansebooks.com**

From "CHRISTIAN THOUGHT,"
Edited by the late REV. CHAS. F. DEEMS, D. D.,
New York, December, 1890.

THE ADAPTABILITY OF REVELATION.

The miracle of a divine revelation appears in its adaptability to every stage of human development. In order to be received at all, it must be clothed in the customs and traditions of the people to whom it is first presented. But as soon as that dress is outgrown, another shows itself beneath, fitted to the advancing growth of humanity.

The Sacred Scriptures do not treat of exact science. They are necessarily written in agreement with the imperfect science of their time. Yet they are capable of accommodation to true science as it becomes known.

What should we *a priori* expect of a composition claiming to be divinely inspired for the instruction of all mankind in all ages? Whatever profound wisdom might be hidden within, to be unveiled in due time, should we not expect that its superficial meaning at least would be clear to those to whom it was first addressed and who were to act as its custodians? Would it, when addressed to a primitive people, express the facts of external nature with the most modern scientific accuracy? For example, when alluding to the familiar fact of sunrise, would it say: the sun being comparatively stationary, and the earth revolving upon its axis, the latter has now reached that position, in its daily rotation, whence the former appears above our horizon? Even the astronomer, unless he be a pedant, speaks, in his ordinary daily intercourse, as though the earth were central to the sun. And we, if wise, for a long time, permit a child to accept the evidence of the senses as indisputable, being satisfied that education will, in due time, correct the fallacies of sense. And ought we to look for less practical wisdom in the Bible, when dealing with the childhood of the race?

When an English missionary wishes to gain access to an untutored savage, does he make use of the English language? He of course first learns the language of the savage. But this is not all. He must translate, not words merely, but the *ideas* he wishes to inculcate into some agreement with the narrow prejudices of his pupil, utilizing for this purpose to some extent, the superstitions already rooted in the mind, and thus gradually leading him to higher conceptions.

Thus is met the objection, that what is called revelation is in large part made up of trivial and commonplace things.

Nearly every one understands the uses of a fable or a parable; though there are infantile minds whose unassisted grasp can barely apprehend literal story. These gnaw at the crude shell without suspecting the nutrient kernel concealed within. But most minds are capable, when their time is ripe, of learning something of "the mysteries of the kingdom of God" by parables. If, then, the Word of God is so wonderfully constructed as to contain parable within parable, until it has an appropriate meaning for every sphere of thought, it may well be called the Book of books.

Next consider the nature and effect of prayer. As God is unchangeable, prayer cannot change Him. But prayer can change the suppliant. It changes his attitude toward God, favorably disposing for the reception of the blessings which are ever ready to flow in their appropriate channels, but cannot flow until prayer opens those channels. In other words, God is the Sun of love and truth, ever shining, ever giving. As mortals turn toward Him they receive the light of life. As they turn from Him they meet darkness and death. Although we know that the sun stands still, while the earth moves, yet we daily speak according to the appearance. So, although we know that God is unchangeable and that all change of relations must be due to change in the dependent creature, yet we continue to pray as though the desired change must be on the part of God. But what harm results? In moments of reflection each will understand according to his capacity, and as the mind expands it will take a wider view and perceive that prayer has only brought it into harmony with unvarying laws. The human mind, in the course of its development from mere animality into the divine likeness, is ever attended by illusive appearances.

The belief that God, being omnipotent, could, if He would, bestow unconditional happiness upon His creatures, is only a natural, popular error. But to suppose, as some seem to suppose, that this heathenish notion of a magical deity is shared by the enlightened teachers of Christianity, is very uncomplimentary to their intelligence. Under such an impression is it any wonder that scientists, whose sole business it is to discover law and trace its effects, should reject Christianity? To conceive that the Author of law and order could Himself act capriciously or with favoritism, is one of those crude primitive beliefs that still linger in regions where mere feeling is allowed to take the place of reflection.

Is it then to be inferred that former interpretations of Scripture were false? By no means. They were in the main true, in their time and place. For man's use truth must always remain correlative to his degree of development. There is no absolutely true creed to which all men could subscribe. As "there is none good but one," so there is none true but one. God is perfect and unchangeable. But unless man changes, he stagnates and rots in the ignorance and folly of his superstitions and prejudices. If Christianity would lead the progress of the race, it must itself be progressive.

Most men wish to have their spiritual affairs settled once for all, and then laid aside, so that they may give up their minds to the real business of their lives, whether that be the pursuit of wealth, or power, or pleasure. But spiritual affairs are never settled. They are always progressive, in spite of the vested interests whose policy is to let well enough alone.

If Christianity be, as it claims, a divine dispensation, it involves truth in all its forms. These it must gradually evolve in the fullness of time; and no genuine truth, however natural or scientific, can claim any other origin or allegiance. Whatever cannot be thus affiliated is falsehood, and comes from the father of lies. To relinquish certain orders of truth to the exclusive custody of science, is a weak abandonment of a sacred trust. All truth belongs to God, and it is all required to complete the outer as well as the inner courts of His temple. The neglect of Christianity to possess and cultivate its entire heritage is responsible for the hostile attitude of infidel science. There is but one source of truth. The stream is pure as it leaves the fountain. But it must be modified by the imperfection and impurity of the vessels into which and through which it flows.

In none of His works is the infinity of the Creator more clearly displayed than in the diversity of created minds; no two being exactly alike.   It is the boast of human invention to construct a machine all of whose products shall be exactly alike.   The glory of the divine creation is shown by the infinite variety of its offspring.   Hence the necessity of correspondingly various creeds and religious observances, and hence the difficulty of preserving uniformity among the professors of the same creed, without the suppression of free inquiry; and hence also the imperative obligation of mutual forbearance.   Men have been reproached and punished for non-conformity as if it proceeded from mere perversity, rather than from the honest exercise of God-given faculties.   Within the limits of fundamental principles this variety of apprehension may be presumed to last to eternity.   When large numbers claim to agree perfectly in opinion, it will be found that most of them have no opinion of their own.   Seeming unanimity is secured by the great majority taking everything on trust; submitting to the dictation of others.   Such are very accurately described as being of the same *persuasion*.

Many photographs of the same object, taken from different points of view, may be all perfect as far as they go.   But the attempt to combine them into one picture, by the process of superposition, would result in nothing but confusion.   Each human soul is a mirror reflecting so much of the divine life as its own separate and partial view permits.   But though each were a true reflection, comparison with other reflections would reveal apparently irreconcilable differences.   And if all could really be brought into the same mind, what a tame universe we should have.   Harmony is not identity.   That would be mere monotony.   True harmony arises from the amicable recognition and proper co-ordination of innate differences; differences which imply imperfection on the part of individual men taken separately; but when taken in orderly combination with other men, these differences illustrate the infinite perfection of the Creator.

The various denominations of Christians, each forming but a fractional part of Christendom, not to mention their still smaller fractional relation to mankind, differ upon some points of doctrine.   And many parents and guardians greatly prefer to have their children and wards exclusively taught their own peculiar views.   But will any rational man claim that one of these denominations possesses the absolute truth to the exclusion of the others? Or that the Infinite Jehovah can be measured and defined by any creed which it is possible for human wisdom to formulate?

But if no two can think exactly alike, and if progress is essential to full spiritual life, how is it that large numbers can subscribe to the same formula, and persuade themselves and others that they fully agree? How, under the dispensation of an all-wise Providence, is this state of things to be accounted for? What important use in the divine economy is subserved by this steadfast, immovable adhesion to a cast-iron creed? To those whose faith in God is without reserve, does it not suggest the vast importance of conservatism? Does it not prove the overwhelming necessity to the average mind of something to which it can cling with unflinching tenacity, as if to prevent a lapse into lower forms of faith, thus maintaining a vantage ground for the further progress of the race?

Progress is for those who have the ability and the courage to think for themselves. Conservatism is for those who permit others to think for them. Among the conservatives, however, are many fully competent to think for themselves. But having, as they imagine, made all secure on the side of religion, they prefer to employ their intellectual forces in more congenial fields. The importance of conservatism is illustrated in the cases of some who have fallen away from the faith of their fathers, without having first provided themselves with something better to take its place. But the true destiny of the race is progress; a progress based upon the sure foundations of the past, but which fears not to build with the new stones of truth, laboriously quarried out of the paths of experience, and shaped by the informing Spirit. But permanent progress will be slow. If a man could be admitted to the secret counsels of the Most High, and, becoming thus acquainted with truths transcending the present reach of human thought, should prematurely disclose them to the confusion of present beliefs; such a man would be an enemy of his kind. God reveals Himself in His own good time. "I have many things to say unto you, but ye cannot bear them now."

When it is promised that the lion shall lie down with the lamb, the prevalence of charity over doctrine is clearly indicated.   Men will agree to disagree intellectually; for the lion will remain a lion and the lamb remain a lamb, their natures brought into due subordination but not destroyed.   Regeneration is a change of *heart*.   The corresponding change of *mind* must take place in accordance with the laws of mind.   What the Christian Church much needs for true progress is reconciliation and co-operation among its various branches.   And in view of inevitable intellectual differences, charity is the only possible ground upon which such reconciliation can take place.

WARREN HOLDEN.

Without designing to provoke a controversy with the author of a late article entitled "If there had been no Race-Lapse," it is here alluded to as furnishing a convenient text for the following remarks.

This "If" seems to imply that the *Fall* was merely a mishap, instead of an essential element or component part of our Race development.

What was the condition from which the Race fell? It accords with a rational conception of Divine Order to regard the Most Ancient Church as the Church in its infancy; very lovely and happy in the obedience of innocence, and very "wise from the Lord": a condition prophetic of the image and the likeness of God to be finally evolved. But was the Race to continue "the stunted nursling of the skies"? The innocence of infancy was gradually* changing into the willfulness of childhood long before the full *flood* of adolescence burst upon the world. Is it mere perversity that makes the growing youth desire "to be wise from himself"? Or is it not rather a part of that far-seeing Providence whose final purpose is to develop full manhood? Consequently we have what *appears* from the human side a most disastrous fall, but which may in the end prove a direct progress through "ups and downs," toward the goal.

Must not the Church, like the Race and the individual, pass through all the intermediate stages of childhood, adolescence, and early manhood, ere it reaches maturity? This obviously seems the Creator's plan. He proposed to create men who should be capable of sympathetic intercourse with himself upon approximately intimate terms. For this end man is endowed with many noble faculties, crowned with freedom and rationality, presumably intended to serve as incentive and guide to self-exertion. What is the use of the above "If" when the Omniscient must have known that such Lapse was inevitable? Freedom and rationality are what mainly distinguish man from the

---

* That the *Fall* was a gradual process, see A. C. n. 502, and what follows.

animal creation, which was perfect in its degree and has remained so Can we conceive the Creator saying in effect to his intelligent creature: This noble crown of freedom and rationality which proclaims your superiority to the beasts that perish, is designed for ornament rather than for use: For if, under its natural inspiration, you dare to act independently, you do so at the peril of your soul? Nothing can develop us into efficient co-workers with the indefatigable Artificer of the Spiritual Universe but the sturdy exercise of freedom according to reason. Bear in mind that man's true creation is effected not from without but from within; that it is a work in which each individual takes an active part; that it extends throughout natural life, and continues in the life to come; and it will be seen that freedom exercised according to reason is an indispensable factor.

It is said that, " Had not the Race lapsed from its first integrity" . . . . . " For this world there would have been no necessity for the Deity to be Incarnated in Human Nature." That being so, *this* world may well be proud of the distinction of being instrumental in bringing about so glorious a consummation, whereby humanity may be lifted to the highest rank of the universe — oneness with the Father of Eternity. " And I, if I be lifted up, will draw all men unto me."

The benefits of redemption through Christ are offered to all. But in the fierce struggle of life — opposition without and passion within — many have been too impetuous in their self-assertion, prompted, perhaps, by a too stubborn independence. Such have fallen into depths of degradation seemingly beyond the utmost reach of mercy's sounding-line. Is there no hope for them? In the far future, among the inexhaustible resources of Infinite Love, as yet unrevealed to us, and after the direst vastations, may not a way be found to restore them to their right mind, and " rehabilitate them in the affections of their fellow men "? And may they not come finally to be recognized as hardy pioneers in the cause of human enfranchisement? Our Lord's visit to Hades to minister to the spirits in prison, lends some color to such a hope.

Why should there be such misapprehensions and such differences of opinion among us? Simply because from the first we are misled by appearances. Accordingly the Lord has told us why he spake in parables; Paul has reminded us that milk is for babes, strong meat for men, and that now we see through a glass darkly. To the reader who bears in mind that during the nonage, whether of the Race or the individual, man's perceptions are necessarily obscured under a cloud of appearances, the more dense the nearer his beginnings, it will be superfluous to weaken the above statements by qualifications which will readily suggest themselves. A proper answer to the question at the head of this article will always depend upon the spiritual age of each.

If ever in the course of his development man could reach God's point of view, the mere appearances which are the necessary accompaniments of his gradual creation into the likeness of his Maker, would no longer obscure his vision, and he would see just as God sees. Then there would be no apparent inconsistencies and contradictions; and the whole course of man's evolution out of mere nothingness and emptiness into a being of miraculous endowments, a creator indeed second only to the Omnipotent; would be disclosed as an orderly progression with nothing wanting and nothing superfluous, a perfect result of harmonious co-operation between the All-wise Father and his beloved son.

It is likely that there are errors in the above. If so, the writer invites, and will be thankful for, candid criticism.

WARREN HOLDEN.

1726 Girard Ave., Philadelphia.

CAN GOD FAIL TO ACCOMPLISH HIS ENDS?

God is infinite love, wisdom and power. Under this defini-
tion, it is only necessary to know the divine purpose in order
to predict human destiny. God's chief aim was and is to create
man in his own image and likeness. This sublime work cannot
be effected by a mere, *fiat*, nor in a day. In man's long and
arduous journey from irresponsible infancy to conscious fellow-
ship with his Maker, all ,the resources 'of both Creator and
gradually developing creature will be called into requisition.
And as the journey of the growing man is made for the most
part under a cloud of illusive appearances, these must color
his vision and modify his attitude toward his great leader. Is
it any wonder that mistakes and falls should be frequent? Are
they not the' stepping stones of progress?

The error of Calvinism lies not in its recognition of God's
foreknowledge and foreordination, since these are essential
elements of the Divine providence; but rather in its hasty
inference from and unwarranted application of these attributes,
whereby He, whose name is Love, is suffered to rest under the
imputation of exercising an irrational despotism which would
disgrace any civilized earthly ruler. Disguising such question-
able dealings under the plea of holiness will never satisfy an
unfettered understanding. Even an unsophisticated child
would repudiate such a travesty of justice.

The self-abnegation which impelled the earlier Calvinists to
accept what seemed to them the logical consequences of their
direful doctrine, even though it should consign themselves to
perdition, attested their sincerity and partook of the heroism
of martyrdom. It must have had an important use to serve in
the divine economy. But that phase has faded away, and the
hereditary receivers of Calvinism, (for there can be no new
converts,) may be divided into three classes. 1st. The vast
majority who take it on trust, leaving its knotty points to theo-
logians, while devoting the best powers of their own minds to
matters with "no relish of salvation" in them. 2d. The tender consciences which suffer a life-long agony between their
fear of offending God and their horror at the helpless doom of
man. These deserve the gentlest human sympathy. And 3d.

A few *elect* who accept the supposed favoritism of heaven as their due, and look with complacency upon the eternal misery of the multitude.   The less said about them the better.

Then inventors of this cruel doctrine, in their impatience to settle the affairs of God's administration for all time, became the dupes of their own hastily and ill constructed logic mill. But "The mills of God grind slowly."

To his own consciousness man is perfectly free, while reflectively he must acknowledge the Divine Supremacy.   This apparent contradiction cannot be reconciled so long as we persist in limiting God by human standards.   When we reduce God to our own dimensions and then reason about our mutual relations, the conclusion must of necessity be fallacious.

"For my thoughts are not your thoughts, neither are your ways my ways, saith the Lord.   For as the heavens are higher than the earth, so are my ways higher than your ways, and my thoughts than your thoughts."   God occupies a higher plane than any of his creatures.   Each in his own plane may enjoy perfect liberty to all appearance, and yet be subject to an unseen control.   To feel free is practically to be free.   So that without any surrender of our proper independence we may acknowledge that

> "There's a divinity that shapes our ends,
> Rough-hew them how we will."

"Behold, the days come, saith the Lord, that I will make a new covenant;   .   .   .   I will put my law in their inward parts, and write it in their hearts.   .   .   .   And they shall teach no more every man his neighbor, and every man his brother, saying, Know the Lord: for they shall all know me, from the least of them unto the greatest of them."   Is not here a sufficient warrant, and a direct invitation to

> "Look in thy heart and write"?

The man who is afraid to trust his own intuitions, deserves to sink into the spiritual imbecility which has hitherto been the self-imposed lot of the vast majority.   The suppression of honest conviction on the part of the many, leaves the vital questions of orthodoxy to be settled by a few.

"In the multitude of counsellors there is safety."   "Quench not the Spirit."   When the Lord has lighted our candle and we put it under a bushel, we not only prevent others from seeing, but snuff out our own perception.   If any refuse to testify, the Lord will choose other witnesses of his truth.   Better the risk of some error, than stagnation.   "The world moves" only as it is impelled by the individual minds which together constitute its life.   As these co-operate with the divine purpose God's Kingdom will cqme, and his will be done on the earth as it is in the heavens.   In the exercise of their freedom men may hasten or delay the grand consummation, but can never finally defeat it.   Final defeat would involve the dethronement of the Deity.   WARREN HOLDEN.

1726 Girard Ave., Philadelphia.

THE COMPLETENESS OF THE DIVINE OVERSIGHT.

"Known unto God are all his works from the beginning of the world."
"The Lord is good to all; and his tender mercies are over all his works."
"What could have been done more to my vineyard that I have not done in it?"

It is a necessary corollary of the Divine character, as made known by external revelation and confirmed by intuitive perception, or internal revelation, that at each successive moment of his life man's opportunities should be the best possible consistently with his indispensable freedom of choice. The Divine providence follows every step of each individual man with a minute attention to his present wants, which would be totally inconceivable except in a being of infinite resources. If one has made a wise use of his opportunities during the past moment, the Lord at once says to him: "Friend, come up higher." But if one has neglected or made an unwise use of the opportunities of the immediately preceding moment, the same watchful providence at once adapts itself to the case as it stands, and says: "Repent, and do the first works." Without such constantly renewed choice on the part of man, he could have no existence in the true sense of that high designation—man. Every attempt to formulate conditions more favorable than those which daily meet him, involves a denial of the prime element of manhood, viz., freedom. We may as well, once for all, concede that God will not stir a finger to obstruct our rational freedom. Such interference would stultify his entire work of creation.

Yet very notable is the tenacity with which we secretly cling to the superstition that God has his favorites, and that *we* are among them. This pernicious falsehood is seemingly countenanced by the literal interpretation of many passages of the Word. And no belief affords more nourishment to human selfishness, meanness and injustice. Hence nothing would do more to clear our moral atmosphere, dissipate false hopes and show us the true path of life, than the practical recognition of God's absolute impartiality.

"Let God be found true, but every man a liar." Whatever doctrine, opinion or inference, drawn from the Sacred Scriptures, is in conflict with the essential characteristics of God, must be false, however logical the deduction appears to be. By selecting passages out of the Bible, suited to the purpose, the most contrary views may be established. But there are prominent statements which rise like mountains above the plane, whose significance cannot be mistaken. These landmarks are recognized by every one. Following their guidance we cannot go far astray. He who runs may read, and "the wayfaring men, though fools, shall not err therein." If this be true, then those passages of Scripture which seem to justify contradictory conclusions, must be misunderstood. Among the lofty peaks seen from every side, is that on which blazes the beacon: "God is love." The search-light of this innermost truth of the universe reveals the true character of whatever comes within its range. Whatever cannot bear and openly reflect its beams, is false.

Yet no two thinking minds can be brought into perfect agreement. Those only seem to agree who do not think for themselves, but allow others to think for them. These do not count here. Perfect unanimity, except in the most general sense, would mean abdication of the manhood which is the inheritance of each. No part of creation so completely vindicates the infinity of the Creator as the mental differences among men. As no two forms or faces are exactly alike, so the minds which these express cannot be identical. Still there may be perfect harmony, where each differs from his near neighbors just enough to produce pleasing variety. Each individual is destined to fill a different niche in the temple of the universe, or the grand man; and hence will differ from others as do the parts and functions of the human body. But a community made up of individuals all cast in the same mold, so that to see and converse with one is to see and converse with any other, would be intolerable both to themselves and to the rest of the universe. The attempts to approximate such a result, which have been made on earth, have proved dismal failures. Whoever aims to bring men into absolute unanimity is the enemy alike of God and man. But any whole made up of harmonious parts is an epitome of heaven.

The doctrine of special providence, implied in the foregoing statements. is a great stumbling block to the natural mind. How can any conceivable administration adapt itself to the myriads of varying conditions? To admit the force of this objection would seem a flat contradiction of all that has gone before. Yet it must be admitted, unless some high ground of reconciliation can be found. And here is the proposed solution of the difficulty: A universal law in the hands of an infinite lawgiver is self-executing, and hence has all the effect of a special interference in each individual case. The principle here involved is operative in the so-called laws of nature. We are prone to overlook the immense difference between infinite and finite, involving as it does the self-administration and execution of divine law. Though to human faculties, as at present developed, this difference is such as to be beyond definite conception, yet the direction in which it tends is plain enough to encourage unbounded confidence in the power and intention of our Heavenly Father to do for us abundantly above and beyond our most sanguine expectations. As the spiritual mind in man is opened, it seems probable that a due consideration of the difference between infinite and finite will furnish a key to many of the mysteries of faith.

WARREN HOLDEN.

LAW AND MIRACLE.

The difference between the advocates of law and the believ-ers in miracle seems based upon the assumption that the two views are irreconcilable. The devout heart bows with rever-ent submission to the obvious teachings of the oracles of God, even when beyond its comprehension. On the other hand, where the rational faculties are allowed to speak freely, they declare the inconsistency of supposing that the Author of law and order could Himself act in direct contravention to His own laws. These antagonistic views may be reconciled by allowing that where revelation attributes to the Creator what seems to contradict rational perception, either the divine power is exercised under a more comprehensive law than has yet been grasped by the human mind, or else the human mind is misled by appearances. So long as miracle is acknowledged to be a real as well as an apparent violation of law, the scien-tific mind cannot help rejecting it. But science seems to assume that somehow certain laws or forces of nature have been set agoing and must thereafter continue in operation of themselves. If, however, it be granted that the life of nature is not inherent, but is continually communicated by the one infinite source of life, it becomes possible to admit further that such life may be controlled in a way not yet familiar to us.

"The wind bloweth where it listeth, and thou hearest the sound thereof, but canst not tell whence it cometh, and whither it goeth. So is every one that is born of the Spirit." To the uninstructed imagination the vagaries of the wind must have seemed among the most mysterious phenomena of nature, and hence the aptness of the above comparison. But modern sci-ence has explored the cave of old Æolus, and revealed all its secrets, so that the same illustration would not be now available.

Let us now consider the most incredible of the miracles, viz., the birth of the Lord Jesus Christ, and see how it stands related to evolution.

No animal or plant has life in itself as its own.   Life is the gift of God wherever manifested; and it is not given once for all, but is imparted moment by moment.   It acts through different organisms and under various conditions, but it is ever the same indivisible force.   The natural sun is the principal medium through which life acts in the physical creation.   Blot out the sun and all nature dies.   But the sun has no life of its own.   Whence comes its force?   Analogy has led astronomers to conceive of a great central sun, the source of all suns.   But in vain would their telescopes sweep the heavens to find it because it is none other than that "bright essence increate" of which every sun in the universe is but an "effluence."   This "coeternal beam" is more intimately present throughout creation than any of its material shadows, the natural rays, can be. "Whither shall I go from Thy Spirit? or whither shall I flee from Thy presence?   If I ascend up into Heaven, Thou art there: if I make my bed in hell, behold, Thou art there.   If I take the wings of the morning, and dwell in the uttermost parts of the sea, even there shall Thy hand lead me, and Thy right hand shall hold me."

The body is from the earth, the spirit is from God.   "Then shall the dust return to the earth as it was; and the spirit shall return to God who gave it."

When life from the All-Father is communicated through the medium of a human father, it is encumbered with his limitations.   But life, communicated directly from its primal source, would be uncontaminated by hereditary bias on the father's side, and the offspring would be prejudiced only by the imperfections of the mother.   Under the former supposition the wonderful intuitive wisdom of Christ, and especially His inconceivable love and divine patience, would be wholly inexplicable.   But under the second supposition all difficulty is removed, and we have Emmanuel—God-with-us.   The Father of eternity is known to us only through His manifestations, the highest of which is Christ.   "No man hath seen God at any time; the only begotten Son which is in the bosom of the Father, He hath declared Him." Life is divine in every sphere. It retains its divine character, whether received indirectly through the species in which it is manifested (and this seems to us the direct method), or whether received directly from God. In both cases its divine character is essential—the *sine qua non* of life. There is no common herd of men. Every man is God's handiwork, never nature's journey-work. Every man has a special place to fill in the grand final outcome, however obscure some may,. for the present, appear. Therefore every man is a special creation. "Known unto God are all His works from the beginning of the world." When it is necessary, in the fulness of time, to pass from a lower to a higher type, the Life which is present in all cases acts directly without the usual intermediate. This direct action of creative energy, occurring when the progress of creation requires, is what science stigmatizes as an interference with the laws of nature; whereas it may more justly be called one of creation's periodic stages.

Bearing in mind that all life is from a single source, both in its beginning and in its continuance, and that every new form of it is a special creation, we may easily conceive that its higher and higher types take their rise by the direct operation of an immanent Creator, and thus we are distinctly told that the highest type of all, the man Christ Jesus, appeared among us. It is one life-giving power acting all the time, not in violation of law, but in strict accordance with a law whose cycle is beyond our unaided ken, but which is plain enough when revealed. Thus every missing link is supplied.

We say that God is omnipresent, but still think and act as if He were far from us. Practically we forget that "in Him we live, and move, and have our being." Omnipresence is not an abstraction, a mere figure of speech. It is the one vital reality. Think of God as the all-pervading life, ever acting in and through His creatures, but at the same time imparting to man His creature *par excellence*, a certain power of resistance or reaction, which constitutes his freedom, the exercise of which develops his individuality. If God be the principal, and man only the secondary, agent in every act of life, it seems easy enough for the principal to give His creation a new direction in the regular course of things whenever His ulterior purposes demand.

Geology may indicate some of the steps, and evolution something of the method of creation, but every act is performed by the Creator Himself. Like the Play of Hamlet with Hamlet left out, modern Evolution undertakes to present the grand Drama of Creation without the chief Actor.

WARREN HOLDEN.

THE SIGNIFICANCE OF DREAMS.

In the ideal community, where equal laws well administered secure to each citizen the largest liberty in harmony with the equal rights of all, freedom is only another name for constant self-control. This self-restraint is imposed by the civil laws, by the rules and regulations of business interests, and by the etiquette of social intercourse. To such an extent does the individual find his course mapped out, that it seems quite impossible for him, however candid he may be, to determine what spirit he is of, and he may easily be led to think of himself more highly than he ought to think. In a word, civilized society fosters unconscious hypocrisy.

But "in thoughts from the visions of the night, when deep sleep falleth on men," in the experience of some persons, these restraints are partly and often wholly removed, and the subject sees his naked self revealed, sometimes in utter disregard of the equities, and even of the decencies and proprieties of life. Upon awaking, in the disgust excited from finding himself, as he claims, an unwilling actor in such a scene, he indignantly exclaims with Hazael: Is thy servant a dog that he should do this thing? And he throws off the unpleasant nightmare with the soothing consolation that it was but a dream, for which he cannot be held responsible.

But is it wise to dismiss a timely warning in this unceremonious way? May it not be made of practical use to a sincere seeker after self-knowledge?

It is related of John Bradford, of London, that whenever he met a condemned malefactor on his way from Newgate to Tyburn to expiate his crimes upon the gallows, he was wont to exclaim: "There goes John Bradford but for the grace of God"; thus acknowledging that, in and of himself, he was no better than the vilest wretch that ever was hung. The Lord confirmed this view when He said: There is none good but One. How, then, can we ever attain goodness? Only by becoming partakers of the divine nature. And how can this be effected? "By grace ye are saved through faith; and that not of yourselves; it is the gift of God."

A devout seeker after holiness thus sang:

" Even in my dreams I'd be
Nearer, my God, to thee."

The gracious soul that realizes this aspiration is not far from the Kingdom of heaven.

When we successfully resist temptation during our waking hours, we may not be able to determine how far mere prudence or the fear of the world's censure ought to be credited with the victory.   But when, during the helpless hours of sleep, we are assailed by evil spirits, and in those trying moments the spontaneous action of the will is such as to invite the assistance of our good angels, so that we are enabled to resist the devil until he flees from us, we may thank God and take courage.

The lesson to be here enforced is that God "hath made of one blood all the nations of men," . . . "In Him we live and move and have our being," . . . "For we are also his offspring."   Hence the boast of the Pharisee, "I am holier than thou," is never justified by fact.

The differences among men, from a spiritual point of view, are merely differences of relation to the one source of life; differences depending upon the degree of voluntary reception of that life.   Freedom of choice forms the chief characteristic of man, as allied to God, and as distinguished from all lower creations.   Therefore, nothing short of annihilation can obliterate our eternal dependence upon an impartial Father.

WARREN HOLDEN.

THE CONNECTION BETWEEN SOUL AND BODY.

Now that the medical profession has recognized Hypnotism as a legitimate therapeutic agent, under the influence of which morbid symptoms may, in some cases, be dissipated by mere suggestion, it seems to follow that sickness must, in such cases at least, be regarded as primarily an affection of the mind or spirit, and only secondarily of the body.

(Mind, soul and spirit are not identical. But when considered in relation to the body, they are almost equally spiritual and the terms are therefore employed indiscriminately in this article.)

The human body is not the man. It is only a material organism through which the human spirit or real man holds intercourse with the visible world and with other men. The body, thus occupying an intermediate position, is acted upon both from without and from within. Many diseases and injuries attack it from without, requiring for their removal the aid of surgery and medicine. But, as intimated above, the cures effected through hypnotic suggestion seem to indicate that other disorders have an inward or spiritual origin, and may be reached by means which, until within a few years, have been stigmatized as imposture. Thus the various forms of mind cure, making due allowance for much charlatanry; the apparently miraculous cures effected at holy places in all ages, the world over, of which the shrine at Lourdes offers a modern instance; and even the conjurations to which the ignorant submit in simple faith; can no longer be dismissed from serious consideration as mere deception practiced upon the credulous, while the patients can exhibit tangible and lasting results of the treatment.

On the other hand, there are well authenticated instances in which serious illness has been brought on by mere suggestion; as also through fear during the prevalence of epidemics. The evil eye, or the supposed malevolent glance of certain outcasts of society, has been followed by real disorders.

Persons who have no time to be sick, are frequently able to throw off incipient disease by an effort of the will; while those who have nothing to do but nurse their symptoms, become confirmed invalids.

In great emergencies what magic power transforms a feeble frame into sinews of steel and nerves of fire, enabling the possessor to execute prodigies of strength? If the extraordinary exertion is succeeded by the lassitude of reaction, that fact serves but to emphasize the difference between soul and body, and to illustrate the dependence of the latter upon the former, which it is the object of this article to show. "It is the spirit that quickeneth: the flesh profiteth nothing."

When compelled to allow rest to the body in sleep, we sometimes become aware of the continual activity of mind in dreams. How often the entrance of a trusted physician lightens the gloom of the sick chamber and brings immediate relief to the patient. Thus a prime function of a physician is to "minister to a mind diseased." With some allowance for poetic licence, we may take the poet quite seriously when he says: "There is nothing either good or bad, but thinking makes it so."

Even the miraculous healings wrought by the touch or word of the Master, in most cases exacted faith on the part of the subject as a condition of success.

"Believest thou that I am able to do this?" "Be it unto you according to your faith." "He did not many mighty works there because of their unbelief."

In general, therefore, it may be said that both sickness and health depend more upon the spirit than upon the body. The spirit is the real man. The body is a mere covering adapted to the conditions of the material world. The material body is the clothing which the spirit wears while exposed to the inclemencies of natural existence, and is no more an inseparable part of the man than the outer clothing is an inseparable part of the body. As we put off the outer garments when we retire to rest at night, so we put off the material body at the sleep of death. "There is a natural body, and there is a spiritual body."

To understand sickness we must know what constitutes health. Health is simply normal relations with the source of life. The unobstructed reception of life from its one divine source constitutes perfect health. But God, the fountain of life, is Spirit; and since the stream, as it issues from the fountain, must be like the fountain, man is at first pure Spirit, however much he may become contaminated afterward. In view of man's parentage and final destiny, the question here arises whether that division of labor, by which the cure of souls has become a separate profession from the cure of bodies, is in the line of true progress. In the future it may be found expedient to reunite the two professions.

The facts, principles and texts here cited, to which many might be added, are all familiar enough, taken separately, but when brought together they afford cumulative evidence of the true relation between soul and body. That is to say, "that *man* is a *spirit*, and that the body serves him for the performance of uses in the world;" the one an eternal reality, the other a temporary appearance.

WARREN HOLDEN.

THE OMNIPOTENCE OF DIVINE LAW.

To childhood, whether of the individual or of the race, Omnipotence means the irresponsible power to do whatever caprice may prompt. To this state of mind it seems irreverent to say that God cannot do what He will with his own. Semi-civilized rulers claim it as one of their prerogatives, inherent in the divine right of Kings, to wrest the law, if they acknowledge any law, so as to protect their favorites and flatterers. But all this is puerile.

To the rational perception of the mature mind God and Law are synonymous terms. Chance, Fate, Doubt, Partiality belong to the dark ages of ignorance and superstition. The certain and uniform action of Law constitutes its beneficence and guarantees our safety under its protection. When we know the Law and obey it, we are masters of our own destiny. Enlightened understanding perceives that God could not if He would, and would not if He could, interfere with the execution of his own Laws. When things turn out differently from our wishes and expectations, we may be sure that such result follows either our ignorance or our disobedience.

When the chemist obeys a prescribed formula, he expects the foreseen result without the shadow of a doubt. And yet there are scientists, so called, who have the fatuity to cast doubt upon not only the wisdom but even the very existence of God's Laws. They call the laws which they recognized the laws of nature. Superficial observers of the outer crust of creation, they do not see that their own immunity from annihilation at the hands of insulted Omnipotence is only another proof of His impartial administration of Law.

Thanks to thy holy name, that Thou art not such as we are; but that Thou wilt continue absolutely obedient to thine own Laws, until man at length learns to follow in Thy footsteps.

But what, more specifically, is the nature of this divine Law? It is a wonderfully minute adaptation of means to the great end of human development. It is the daily Providence which creates man through man's own co-operation. It follows him through all his devious wanderings more closely than his shadow, ever ready to help him when he is ready to receive . help, but never forcing his inclination.

"If I ascend up into heaven, Thou art there: if I make my bed in hell, behold, Thou art there.   If I take the wings of the morning, and dwell in the uttermost parts of the sea; even there shall Thy hand lead me, and Thy right hand shall hold me."

Thus a fundamental Law of creation is the inviolate freedom of the human will, which God will never infringe, though the stubborn subject choose to take the untold ages of eternity to come into his right mind.

WARREN HOLDEN.

There have been many interpreters of rules for the right conduct of life, from Solomon down to Emerson. These rules are very comprehensive, if not sometimes a little contradictory.— But for the Christian there is one general rule including all others, viz: the example and teaching of our Lord Jesus Christ.

If it be objected that he spake and acted in accordance with the crude civilization and imperfect science of his time, it may be answered that were he now here he would adapt himself to present circumstances, as indeed he does in the persons of his intelligent disciples.

In times of great perplexity we may ask: how would the Lord meet this case? and we may confidently expect light to appear. And considering that he was tempted in all points as we are, we need not hesitate to appeal to his sympathy in our lowest needs and in our vilest temptations. As he stretched forth his hand to save Peter, so will he rescue us when the boisterous billows of doubt seem ready to swallow us up.

Keep the Lord always in view. There may be moments of intense absorption in some profound problem when all other conscious thoughts will for the time be shut out. But even then unconscious guidance may lead us, and upon looking up from our pre-occupation, the bright oriflamme of the divine presence will flash consciously before the spiritual vision, and the faithful soldier of the cross will be ready again to follow wherever it may lead.

In youth the writer once asked the advice of an honored teacher as to the practicability of literally obeying the injunction to "pray without ceasing." The answer was: You are here to obtain an education, and that prime object should engage your undivided attention during the allotted hours of study. Though few will dispute the wisdom of this advice, yet to the writer its acceptance has always been a subject of regret, as he now believes that there may be an undercurrent of prayer which will not seriously interfere with the most absorbing study. Indeed he had one teacher who could write a letter and carry on a conversation at the same time; a clear illustration of the practice here advocated.

If in great emergencies one will look immediately to the Lord, that friend who sticketh closer than a brother, courage and guidance will be given him to act in a manner becoming the highest heroism. Also in minor straits, when liable to act upon sudden impulse, a timely prayer may restore presence of mind, and save us from mortification and humiliating repentance.

When a sufficient number of disciples are ready to live and act solely in view of eternal interests, the time of the world's redemption draweth nigh. Of course this happy consummation need not be looked for until selfishness, in all its insidious forms, has in their case at least been obliterated. These impartial missionaries will regard their fellow men, even the most degraded, as future temples of the Holy Ghost, only waiting that cleansing and consecration which must be effected in part through their brotherly ministration and co-operation. To them there is nothing common or unclean in its inmost core and ultimate destination.

When the Lord cometh will he find faith on the earth? Never can he come in fulness until faith abounds. When Christians come to believe the glorious promises of the Gospel as implicitly and as practically as many of the heathens believe their fantastic doctrines, the millenium will be upon us. To some extent it rests with us to determine whether the twentieth century shall have the honor of ushering in that acceptable year of the Lord.

WARREN HOLDEN

THE SPIRITUAL WORLD MAN'S TRUE DOMICILE.

In Kentucky, some years ago, an outrageous crime was committed. The guilty man, in order to divert suspicion from himself, headed a mob which lynched an innocent person as the supposed criminal. The victim, thought to be dead, was left hanging from the limb of a tree. A good Samaritan, passing that way, cut him down and resuscitated him. The revived man related a remarkable experience which had occurred to him during the suspension of animation. Now had he not been restored to what we commonly understand by consciousness, this experience would naturally have continued, and formed part of his post-mortem existence. Hence it may be inferred that as soon as external life was suspended, he must have been in the Spiritual world.

During what we erroneously call the unconscious state of sleep, we sometimes have very vivid dreams. The scenes about us are often quite different from our surroundings while awake. We see and converse with persons before unknown to us; we imbibe new ideas, and at times receive warnings which may prove of great importance. Are we not then in the Spiritual world?

Even when so far awake as to exercise full control over our intellectual faculties, we may become so absorbed in some purely mental exercise as to be wholly oblivious of physical existence. Where are we then but in the Spiritual world?

In daily business or social intercourse, we alternate between the inner and outer courts of our being, deliberating with ourselves in secret as to how much of our real mind it may be prudent to divulge openly. Are we not then passing and repassing the portals of the Spiritual world? Are we not *always* essentially spirits, retiring frequently to our private domicile, where we may put off the disguises which we find convenient for public wear?

Persons are sometimes seen going along the street talking earnestly with themselves. When such persons are said to be talking with the devil, the statement may contain more truth than jest.

Referring to Dr. Johnson's intense desire to see a veritable ghost, Carlyle remarked: Why, the good doctor was himself a ghost.

From the above illustrations it follows that the inner or spiritual man is the real man; and that what we permit to come to public view is for the most part mere appearance. It may be true or it may be false appearance, but it is ever changing, and largely dependent upon others. But within the veil is the true man, known only to himself and to his God.

We are in the habit of speaking of the spiritual world as if we had to leave our present condition and *go* somewhere to reach it. Whereas it is in us and about us all the time, being in fact our daily habitation.

WARREN HOLDEN.

www.ingramcontent.com/pod-product-compliance
Lightning Source LLC
Chambersburg PA
CBHW032138080426
42733CB00008B/1119